What people **[barcode]**
You Are Not

*****
This fantastic little book makes a big impact. A must read for those wanting to know what mindfulness is really all about and how to easily bring that into their lives. Every teenager needs a copy of this, probably most adults too.
Olivia Buxton, *Mail On Sunday Health*

I love this book. This level of simplicity and clarity is a tremendous achievement.
Zen Master Daizan Skinner Roshi, author of *Practical Zen*

There are thousands of books out there to help us combat our inner self-destructive voice... some good, some not so good... if I could go back in time and read only one book on the subject, this is it... Frances Trussell has the answer... trust yourself with this book... and trust Frances... everything you need is here... at your fingertips... and the most amazing thing is... it was there all the time! Let Frances guide you to it!
Joe Pasquale, Comedian and Actor

As a how-to-do guide this book contains everything you need to know. Useful for anyone who needs to learn to live in the moment, the techniques and method taught by Frances are easily implemented.
Marisa Peer, leading International Celebrity Therapist and Bestselling Author

You Are Not Your Thoughts

The Secret Magic of Mindfulness

You Are Not Your Thoughts

The Secret Magic of Mindfulness

Frances Trussell

BOOKS

Winchester, UK
Washington, USA

First published by O-Books, 2018
O-Books is an imprint of John Hunt Publishing Ltd., 3 East St., Alresford,
Hampshire SO24 9EE, UK
office1@jhpbooks.net
www.johnhuntpublishing.com

For distributor details and how to order please visit the 'Ordering' section on our website.

Text copyright: Frances Trussell 2017

ISBN: 978 1 78535 816 6
978 1 78535 817 3 (ebook)
Library of Congress Control Number: 2017951931

A CIP catalogue record for this book is available from the British Library.

Design: Stuart Davies

Printed and bound by CPI Group (UK) Ltd, Croydon, CR0 4YY, UK

We operate a distinctive and ethical publishing philosophy in
all areas of our business, from our global network of authors to
production and worldwide distribution.

Contents

Introduction

There's a quiet revolution going on, people everywhere are beginning to wake up from the daydream of their thoughts. All around eyes are blinking into the light of consciousness where millions have chosen to show up and be more present in their lives. Perhaps you are already living this way, or have had a glimmer of how it feels to be truly awake to the reality of the right here and now.

I was depressed, painfully, sometimes suicidally so, for as long as I could remember. Most people wouldn't have necessarily known this as I happen to be a fantastic actor, but that's what it was – an act. I was a fraud. My life outwardly appeared a story of success; I found academic achievement easy, my career took off, I had a wide circle of friends and a wonderful partner, I had nothing to feel miserable about. And yet my inner world was a mess. I was wracked with anxiety, a constant feeling of dread pervaded every part of my life, it would sit on my chest and wake me in the night. I was an over-thinker and cycles of rumination would spin faster and faster around my mind. This spin would weave intricate stories about others' opinions of me or write contingency plans for the many disasters that were just about to occur. It would retell stories, rewriting conversations and old events, dredging up emotions from the bed of the past that would engulf me in a murky fog of sadness. Behind a fixed smile and great shoes I lived constantly in the worlds of past and future that only by getting 'out of my head' on drink and drugs could I seem to escape. I was my thoughts and my thoughts were me, my thoughts were the facts that my reality was built on. Thick, heavy and persistent thinking smothered me repeatedly until I could no longer breathe. I was addicted to the sound of my own voice rumbling around my head, the deafening echoes of my opinions, beliefs and judgements, judging other people

1

and usually most harshly myself. Lost within the confines of a solid skull everything I looked out on through sober eyes was grey and dark and boring.

When I finally 'got' mindfulness it was like someone had flicked a light on; the world that had been dull now shined vividly and vibrantly in full fabulous technicolor. I was astonished that something so simple contained the power to change everything. I wrote this book so that people have to spend less time fumbling around in the dark, and as the light begins to fade (which it will) they will remember where to find the switch.

There's a filter on our experience of this life and that filter is our thoughts, luckily it's all an illusion. Once we know the truth of things for ourselves we really can live more freely and be genuinely happier.

This is just a little book, purposely so, look beyond the letters, take your time to feel what the words point to. Breathe and enjoy. It is easy to miss the most important message of mindfulness, the miracle hiding in plain sight. So here it is, let me share with you the secret magic of mindfulness – You Are Not Your Thoughts.

You Are Not Your Thoughts: Diving into the Heart of Mindfulness

You are not the voice inside your head.

There is a gap, a space, a silence when that voice shuts up.

And this is a space worth exploration.

So put down all judgement and come diving with me.

Letting go of the world of things.

Together let's plunge beneath the surface of separation into the vast pool of absolutely everything.

Here you come home to who you really are.

It's a lovely place to live and it's all here right now.

Mindfulness is having your **mind full** of the thing you are doing right now in this moment.

Do you find that your mind is usually 'somewhere else' worrying about the future, regretting the past, reliving conversations that have already taken place? You are not alone; most people are rarely in-the-moment.

We spend so much of our time lost up in our heads whilst 'out there' our lives are passing us by. When we fail to engage in the fullness of life we can get left with a feeling of emptiness, a void which we try to fill with stuff and people and achievements, yet it is a hunger that cannot be satisfied from the outside in.

When we have our mind full of the experience of life rather than our thoughts we can change the way we feel about our lives for the better. Stop thinking about what might make you happy and start living; you just might find that happiness is already here.

The majority of what we 'think' are thoughts we've had before, the same old, same old, going around in our heads. This kind of repetitive thinking serves no purpose, except to drive us mad.

So how do we get our minds to stop over-thinking and make room for some happiness? We need to swap some of our basic beliefs for new ones, so find some quiet…

Living in the flow

Usually we are at our happiest when we are doing the things that put us 'in the zone', things that are so absorbing we don't have space to think at the same time. If you try to remember your happiest moments it is unlikely to be those when you were lost in thought but rather lost in what you were doing.

When we do something that absorbs our full attention this frees us from thought and it is in these moments, without internal commentary, that we are truly ourselves. You have the power to switch off the subtitles and experience life in flow, you have just forgotten how.

Read this book and retrain your mind to return to the now.

Slow down, be here

What's the rush?

Where are you going?

If you're one of the lucky ones your destination is old age and death.

If your mind is always rushing to be in the future and you hear yourself thinking 'when I do that I'll be happy, when I have achieved that I will be fulfilled' you could find yourself at the end of the road thinking 'what happened to my life?'

Now is all there is

The past is a series of memories and the future hasn't happened yet.

The past, good or bad, has already happened; there is nothing you can do to change it.

Every time you think about it your brain invents new versions of events, thinking back adds fuel to any negatives and this causes an emotional reaction in your body. Your body does not know the difference between a memory and a something happening to you right now. Each time you relive negative experiences from your past you get a rush of feelings and adrenalin; if you do this a lot you live in a state of stress of 'fight or flight' not to real dangers but to thoughts; this is not good for anyone.

Even good memories can trick us into thinking that 'life was better then' and now is not as good. This can stop us from fully committing to or enjoying the present moment. It can also leave us with a sense of loss once the good feeling of the memory subsides and a longing sets in.

The future does not exist, it hasn't happened yet and we have no idea what will happen. We might think we know what's going to happen, we might make guesses, we might worry and again set off a series of chemical reactions in our body. But the future is in the future so who knows; thinking about it is just a distraction from what is actually going on now, right now, and that's all you can ever be sure of.

Being is to be free... of worry, of regret

Once we accept that now is all there is you can just let those things go.

Those regrets are just stories, coulda-woulda-shoulda's that never happened.

Those worries are imagined inventions. They haven't happened and even if they all did, will worrying about them have made any difference?

When we 'be' where we are right now with the fullness of our attention we set ourselves free.

That probably sounds too massive to believe; it's not easy but it is simple. To carry on listening to a voice inside your head that is not you, about a bunch of stuff that is not the reality of your life right now is madness.

Become a master of yourself

You are the only one you are in charge of.

No matter how hard you try you can't control the universe, things will happen in your life, good and bad, much of which you can do nothing about. You can, however, do something about the way you respond to life's events and that all starts in your head.

Now is your opportunity to learn the patterns of your own mind.

Make a start

It all starts without you really having to do much at all, just observe your mind. Let's sit here and just wait for a little thought or comment to come along.

Wait for it.

You might have to wait ages or you may have lots of thoughts instantly pouring in, just observe what happens.

Don't do anything, just watch the thought arise.

What does your mind want to do, jump on it and start thinking? Or maybe because we are bringing our attention to it you can just let the thought go?

Just observe for a while and after you've been able to observe a thought I will meet you on the next page.

Consciousness

Welcome to a new way of experiencing your life.

As soon as we start to watch our thoughts we recognise that we are separate from them. We become conscious that we are instead able to sit as the observer of thoughts, and much more besides.

We are bigger than the smallness of thought and vaster still than a simple observer.

It is then we realise how mad we've been, that there is a voice or voices inside our heads which for all these years we have been listening to. Once you have recognised this there is no turning back; how can you allow yourself to continue to be bossed around and made to feel terrible by a voice inside your head which is not you?

You no longer will – you are free.

Keep watching

From time to time throughout your day tune in to watch your thoughts, see if you can notice them arrive and still stay separate to them.

See if you can notice your urge to engage with a thought and turn it into thinking. See if you can instead watch the thought come and go. If you can't then try just observing where the thought wants to go; you may see patterns emerging, or notice whether these are new thoughts or thoughts you've had before.

Often the simple act of bringing awareness to your thoughts 'breaks the spell' of the thought and it becomes far easier to let it go. When we start to recognise repetitive thoughts we can see how we have just got into a habit of thinking about certain things or in certain ways.

Thoughts are just thoughts, don't judge them or worry about them; that's all just creating more thinking.

The Great Disappearing Act

To believe we are our thoughts is the greatest trick of the mind.

When thought stops where do you go? Is it that you disappear into a puff of smoke?

Or is that when the real you has the space to be magically revealed?

Mind the Gap

Cultivate a 'not minding' attitude to life.

Don't sweat the little stuff by not engaging the mind in it. Once we give ourselves space between thoughts and engaging in thinking then we can choose what we 'mind' about.

When we are operating on autopilot we automatically react to stressors:

Stressor > Reaction

When we bring our awareness to what is going on for us, we give ourselves the opportunity to notice when we are in a potentially stressful situation, be aware of our thoughts, feelings and what is going on in the body.

By switching from autopilot to manual we create a space in which we can choose to respond rather than react:

Stressor > Gap > Response

With our mindful awareness we get to 'mind the gap' between an event and our reaction, hopefully choosing to respond rather than react.

Be here now

Start to focus on the present moment.

What are you doing right now?

I am typing, you are reading.
　　I can feel the keypad beneath my fingers and hear it clicking away.
　　Are you holding a book or a tablet? Can you feel its texture or its warmth?
　　Are you sitting or lying down?
　　Can you feel your body against a chair?
　　How does it feel to be right here where you are?
　　Are there any sounds in the room around you? What can you smell?
　　What is the temperature where you are?
　　Can you feel the fabric of your clothes against your skin?

Don't judge any of these things, just feel them, experience them. If thoughts arise that's OK but as soon as you realise you've been distracted by them just return to your present moment.

Guess what? You're alive and this is what it feels like to be alive in this moment.
　　That's mindfulness.

Feelings are just like the weather

Some days are stormy, others drizzle and sometimes the sun burns so bright it stings your eyes.

There is lots of weather and it is always changing. We can try and predict it but we can't change it; it's just the ebb and flow of nature and its elements.

In Britain we love to obsess over the weather, we talk about it endlessly, comparing it to what went before, what might happen in the future and judging it with terms like 'miserable'.

Weather is just weather, resisting whatever it is, complaining about it, fighting it makes no difference, it's still going to do exactly what it's supposed to – that is to be as it is, however that is. If instead of judging it we just watch, just accepting it as it is, we can find new beauty in all of its guises. It is only when we let it bother us that it bothers us at all.

When we learn to pay attention to the impermanence of life both externally and internally we are less hard on ourselves and our environment. It will usually blow over.

Thoughts are in your head, Feelings are in your body

Thoughts and feelings are very different things. Learn to separate them out and you will soon notice a change in the way you react to them.

When we think we produce feelings; when we worry with our thoughts a feeling of anxiety arises in the body. If we isolate the original thought and learn to separate ourselves from that by recognising it is not reality, it is not something which is happening right now, we can stop the feeling of anxiety developing in the first place. To be able to master this takes some training but observing your thoughts and getting back in touch with reality by paying attention to where you actually are allows a space between thought and feeling to grow.

Face it and feel it

There is nothing in this world that can happen to you which can't be made worse by thinking about it. To really deal with the events of our lives we need to face them and feel them rather than creating lots of thinking around them.

How do you feel?

Throughout your day check in on how you feel. Are you feeling light and free? Do you have a knotted feeling in your stomach? Are your palms sweaty or is there pressure on your chest?

Does any physical feeling sit alongside an emotion? Are you feeling relaxed? Fearful? Excited? Angry?

What has caused this feeling to arise? Is there something happening in this moment to cause it or is your body reacting to thoughts you've been having?

Thoughts have the power to cause a physical feeling to develop in the body. As we become aware of this relationship we can explore our role in feeding thoughts with a compassionate curiosity.

Under the light of awareness we see the possibility of a new type of relationship, a partnership of understanding and connectivity. This light may at times dim, obscured when we drift into distraction. Yet its shine can be brightened as we simply remind ourselves that the quality of our attention is the source of energy feeding this.

Feeling stressed?

If you find yourself feeling stressed then you have some options:

1) you can engage in thinking around the feeling and witness how that usually increases the feeling
2) you can try returning your attention to something in the present moment, an object, a sound, your breath and see if the feeling disappears
3) you can focus on the feeling itself, locate it in the body and feel it rather than think about it and see how it changes

The first option seems to be both unhelpful and a waste of time. So it's up to you to decide whether to distract yourself or deal with the feeling head-on depending on what is more appropriate to the situation you find yourself in. We can very quickly retrain our minds using this technique.

Own your emotions

Your emotion belongs to you. The words or actions of others may leave you feeling incredibly angry, but your anger is you being angry – you are the one that carries that around, you are the one it makes feel bad. Once we recognise emotions as our own, alongside watching our thoughts, we can see when we are adding fuel to those emotions through our thinking.

Stressors will be stressors but it is our stress.

We've all had times that we've 'lost it' where an emotion has erupted from inside us and we have lost control of ourselves in some way; what if you never had to do that again? If we can put some distance between our thoughts and feelings, watching them as they arise, then we have a chance to catch an emotion before it takes us over; to witness it instead of reacting to it. It is not that the emotion shouldn't be there, to feel is human, but as developed humans we have control of our actions.

Emotion is what makes us human

It is totally normal to feel the full range of emotion – that's how we experience the full spectrum of what it is to be alive. Yet we deny ourselves the full human experience by turning away from anything uncomfortable; rather than accepting uncomfortable emotions we resist them and attempt to cure them, creating instead a continuous state of 'wanting'. In the Western world we rarely accept hunger or pain, seeking a constant condition of comfort; the underlying purpose of our lives becomes one of maintaining this condition and yet we are left with an emptiness.

We can blame other people for making us feel bad, however, it is our reaction to them that made us feel bad. You can catch this as it occurs, recognise the thinking this has caused and decide how you want to think and as a result how you feel. Often we have no power over something which happens but we do have power over the way we react, or hopefully respond; this is our greatest power and the way we exercise this will shape our journey through life.

There is no path to happiness, happiness is the path, and it is in every step along our way.

Use your energy wisely

When you feel an emotion rising in the body surrender to where you are now and accept it. When we resist an emotion, that only causes us more pain. If the emotion has already arrived there is no point resisting it or thinking about it, instead just feel it.

You can go about making changes but you can't change what has already happened so don't use your energy to fight that, accept it, move on.

It may sound a difficult thing to do but we need to accept all of the emotions which arise in the body. When we run away from an emotion it chases us and like it or not it will catch up with us eventually.

Stop running, sit still and allow your emotions to be as they are. Once we sit with it we transform it.

BOOM – you don't need to be afraid any more.

Sit with it

We've been retraining ourselves to pay attention to what's going on inside ourselves by:

Watching our thoughts
Separating our thoughts from our feelings
Locating our feelings in the body and feeling them

Now what about what is going on out there in the world?

You are here

You are here right now in this moment.

Be aware of where you are. Without having to do anything or judge anything just notice the space around you.

Notice your body, notice your breath.

Notice how it feels to be alive.

Stop thinking, start living

Mindfulness is... the art of paying attention.

As a young child we are naturally absorbed with the thing we are doing and live in the moment; however, as we grow up our thoughts take over, we get far too clever to concentrate on just one thing at a time and the 'multitasking mind' sets in. Before long we all found ourselves watching TV, while eating, doing our homework and having a conversation and that was without the added distractions of social media that are faced today.

To be completely devoid of thought all the time would be both impossible and impractical. However, the more we live with our minds full of the present, absorbed in the moment, then the thoughts we do think often have a greater clarity and purpose. For those thoughts that don't we are conscious of their nature. We can therefore separate out the nonsense, recognising thoughts that are a good or bad idea. We can act upon worthwhile thoughts and stop ourselves before we turn a bad idea into a bad action. When we practise mindfulness we are less likely to be swept along by thoughts into damaging behaviour and more likely to recognise useful ideas and follow these moments of clearness and creativity through.

Does a mindful life mean a better life?

Once we are conscious of our thoughts we get to choose our actions, shaping outcomes in a conscious rather than unconscious direction.

Will your life be better as a result? Well that depends on what you see as better and how you view your life. Your life is this moment and it is a series of moments that make up your life.

Life is flowing through you right now. You. Here. Now.

The force of life is the same for us all, it is just the situations we find ourselves in that create difference.

In tapping into the breath we awaken to the life that's flowing through us, we make the unconscious conscious. This is why the breath is a keystone of mindfulness.

It doesn't matter where you were born, what you look like, how much money you have or what you believe – we all breathe to live. This is something that our bodies do for us without ever having to think about it and by accessing the breath we tune into this human universality; it is something we all always have access to.

Just Breathe

Just take a few moments to notice the breath. Be absorbed by it, how and where it comes into the body, how it feels, where it goes and how it leaves again.

Breathe.

You can't breathe in the past or the future, only now.

It is always a way you can make a connection with the present moment.

Conscious breath allows us to step back from our thoughts, feelings and reactions.

We can literally 'make some breathing space'.

Observe

Don't try and resist your thoughts, let them come, just know they are not you.

You will notice their patterns and probably find another voice in your head which now answers those thoughts with, 'Hello thoughts, not you again – we have been here already. You are not me.'

Notice a thought, take a conscious breath, then feel how and where any emotion arises in the body.

Still here?

Come back to the present moment; if you have noticed thoughts arriving now let them go by refocusing on this moment.

Breath is a key to this, notice your breath and focus on it fully so that you allow any thought to float away.

Then repeat this process… what you will find is that as you do this through your day and your week and into your life you will notice bigger gaps appearing between thoughts. Now you can immerse yourself more fully into each thing you are doing; in turn you are less filled with negative emotions and more 'at peace'. It is in this peace where pure happiness lies.

Be in Peace

The background of peace – behind comment, behind noise, behind even the silence – this is the indescribable hum of happiness that is ever present.

We shouldn't wait until we are dead to 'rest in peace'; this peace is within us throughout our lives, we just need to pay attention to it.

Right now there are no problems

Right now what problems do you have?

Before you answer lose all thought of the past, lose all projection of the future (neither exist); now faithfully answer right now – in this moment – do you have any problems?

We all have issues in our life situation, we may be dealing with strong emotions around grief or loss but when we examine in the moment what it is that's holding us back from feeling peace it is rarely a real problem, it is usually ourselves. Even if we recognise a genuine 'problem' it is not the problem which makes us feel bad; it is our thoughts about that problem which generate our feelings about it. When we learn to not be controlled by our thoughts we change our feelings and in turn we are able to deal with genuine problems far more efficiently. Problems become things not to be feared but just part of the ebb and flow of life, obstacles to overcome, not resisted or fought or over-thought.

If you are sitting somewhere reading this book chances are many of your problems are 'first world problems'; this is not to say that the emotions which they generate are not strong, painful and destructive but before you allow your mind to tear you apart over them put them into a wider world perspective – this may help you to allow yourself to let them go.

With practice we loosen the grip of destructive thoughts, with this we lessen the problems we are creating in our minds and are left with space in which to be.

Practice might not make perfect (but it reveals the beauty of imperfection)

There is no dress rehearsal for life; this is it, right now. So how on earth do we make the most of it? We can practise adopting the right frame of mind to set us up for dealing better with what gets thrown at us, being more open to people, places, situations, handling our emotions with care and ultimately having the capacity for more joy. This practice is meditation.

For some of us meditation may feel 'new age' or in some way religious and our egos can run wild with this, cue the thoughts 'this is for hippies... what will people think... this isn't the kind of thing I do.'

Well we have already established that these thoughts aren't you, they are a voice in your head, a voice that you can help to quiet through meditation, so you decide. What is more stupid, listening to a voice constantly criticise you or taking some time out to focus and clear your mind? Do you care what people think? If we know that most of our own thoughts are likely to be irrelevant then how can what anyone else thinks be any more relevant?

If the idea of meditation makes you feel uncomfortable, then don't think of it; it's your thoughts that create the feeling of discomfort not the meditation itself. Listen to the 'chatter' that surrounds your discomfort, recognise that those thoughts are not you and let them come and go. Plus 'meditation' is just a word, a label.

Meditation helps you focus on the now so that this can then be carried through to the rest of your life. It sets your intention to be mindful and reminds us how refreshing this can be. Plus it has many health benefits which it's not the purpose of this book to go on about but that hundreds of recent scientific studies can testify to.

There is a space that exists beyond the world we've constructed from concepts, this reality we've built with bricks of words. Meditation is a key that unlocks the door to this space.

Trains of Thought

Trains of thought race through your mind, taking you on a journey to far-off realms in the worlds of past and future thinking. Crossing the frontiers of time and space, moving between reflection and projection, echoes of what may have been and what might still.

There have been times in my life I felt helplessly propelled from one train of thought to the next, often without any awareness but sometimes with an aching sense that I was headed in the wrong direction.

For me, meditation has been like learning to sit at the station. Trains will come, but I know I can choose to stay where I am.

Meditation made easy

You don't need a special mat, cushions, particular clothes, incense or music with monks chanting in the background. All you need is you right now, where you are. You may want to get comfy (not too comfy as falling asleep is a slight hazard); it might help to be somewhere quiet where you are unlikely to get disturbed, although you can actually do it anywhere.

You can either just do it for as long as you feel is right at the time or use a timer so there are some more set parameters to work within. The rest is up to you; for a taster you could start with just 5–10 minutes and see how you get on.

Find somewhere to do it and I'll see you on the next page.

Meditation: Counting the Breath

Relax; you don't have to try very hard. The point is relaxed awareness; that rather than your focus being on your thoughts it is just on this moment in time.

Read the below through once and then when you are ready to give it a go:

Count your breaths 1–10.

In-breath is 1

Out-breath is 2

In-breath is 3

All the way up to 10

And then start again.

You may find it helpful to close your eyes while you do this.

Focus on the breath and the counting and see if you can continue to pay attention to the breath and the number you are in.

Don't rush to get to the next breath or the next number, just be focused on where you are.

Thoughts will pop into your head, that's OK, but as soon as you realise that you have been distracted by a thought just return to counting the breath.

Don't worry if your in-breaths or out-breaths are in a different order to mine, that makes no difference. Don't worry if you lose it after 6 or suddenly find yourself on 16. We are retraining the mind to pay attention and if you are someone with a busy mind then this may feel a bit strange at first. Try to not get frustrated; when thoughts appear just watch them come and watch them go again when you return your attention to counting the breath.

Give it a go.

How was that for you?

Often when we start out meditating we question whether we are doing it right; meditation is very simple and the very act of doing it means that you are doing it right. It is called a practice and we are just practising paying attention, no one is there to judge us on it and the more of it we do the more relaxed with it we become.

Well done, you just started training your mind to be more focused on the present moment.

The more you practise this the more clarity you will create in your mind. Throughout the rest of the book we will look at some different meditation techniques so that you can try these out, mix things up and develop a practice that works for you.

Thinking about the breath

Your breath is natural, you breathe all the time without having to be conscious of it; just because you are focusing on it during the meditation don't worry about it. I find to get myself into a relaxed state of breathing I take a few deep breaths at the start of the exercise then let the breath settle down to a natural breath. It is often helpful at the beginning of the exercise to imagine the deep breaths travelling all the way down into your stomach rather than working with shallow breaths that sit up on your chest.

To guide the deep breath you may want to place your hands on your stomach and feel the rise and fall that happens there. Just notice the deepest point that the breath reaches and invite the breath to draw down a little more.

If you start over-thinking about the breath try to focus more on the numbers as you count. Our breath is usually irregular with the length and depth of each breath altering from the last; none of these things are anything to worry or think about, just something we can place our attention in. It is also quite normal that when we really relax the breath can become so faint it feels like it almost disappears; again this is fine, just be with it and follow it.

There is no right or wrong way of breathing, you are alive so you are breathing and it is something which takes care of itself.

Outside distractions

You may have found that outside noises seemed intense or distracting. Don't resist any noise, just accept it, focus on counting the breath and watch any thoughts around you, noticing noise come and go.

For most of us when we first start meditating it is totally alien to us to have our eyes closed whilst we are awake. It sounds obvious but when you close your eyes it really heightens all of your other senses. We can actually use this as a meditation in itself, a way of connecting with the moment.

Read this through first and then close your eyes to experience a few moments of mindfulness:

> With your eyes closed what can you hear?
>
> First the close sounds then those more distant, different layers of noise that it is possible to experience all at the same time.
>
> Perhaps you can hear a plane, the wind through the trees, a bird, some cars, a child shouting?
>
> Maybe you can hear and feel your breath coming in and out of your body. Experience how the breath feels around your nostrils or lips. You may notice there is a taste in your mouth.
>
> How does your skin feel, is there a breeze, what's the temperature?
>
> Experience the feeling of your feet on the ground or the pressure of your body on the chair.
>
> What can you see with your eyes closed? Are there any colours, shapes or dots?
>
> Where do you stop and the space around you start?

Take a few moments or as long as you want to connect to what it is to be where you are now with your eyes closed and then try to maintain this level of awareness while you slowly open your eyes again, look and really see what is in front of you.

Positioning

Many people find that sitting upright with a straight back and neck and relaxed shoulders really helps them to stay focused during meditation, others like to be lying down either on their back or lying on their right-hand side.

For laying down meditation I like to lie in 'semi-supine' on my back, knees up hip-width apart with a book or block under my head. This is a great way of realigning the spine, plus if you start to drift into sleep your knees wobble to wake you up!

Whatever works for you is fine, just try out some different positions and make sure you are comfortable.

How am I supposed to feel?

Sometimes when we meditate we will experience pure bliss and joy, other times it will be frustration, anger and boredom plus every emotion in-between; it doesn't matter what comes up, the point is to practise being there for whatever arises. This teaches us so much about ourselves and prepares us for dealing with life.

You are supposed to feel however you are feeling.

One Taste

Each moment of life has its own unique flavour. Meditation allows us to dine on this experience directly. A moment arrives with a flavour we like so we grasp at it, trying to suck it in and as we do so it disappears. A bitter moment of meditation comes and we try to spit it out, push it away and so the intensity of this taste grows.

We see how that grasping, clinging and pushing away interferes with what is. In the moments that we simply taste, without judgement, we allow the subtle notes of the next moment to arise like flavoursome soup.

Mind full or mind empty?

Meditation is not about creating a space of non-thought; it is more about realising that this space already exists within you.

Next time you do your counting the breath meditation see if you can notice the gap in between each number. If you can just notice it without commentary or thinking then you will have experienced that space.

That space doesn't go anywhere; it is like the present moment – always there. That space is constant regardless of whatever is arising.

A clear mind is not a destination that you reach through meditation. If when we meditate we just allow whatever is there to be, then everything settles down to reveal itself for what it really is.

Busy mind?

Even when we feel like meditation is not working, it's working.

When we have a 'terrible' meditation where we are constantly distracted, the way that we notice the distraction and the thoughts that are distracting us can be really revealing about the way our minds work and how we can retrain them.

If we persevere in meditation despite a busy mind this may not be as comfortable as when we have a quiet mind but can be really rewarding. As we teach ourselves not to engage with the busy mind we set out our intention to let things be as they are without placing too much importance on our thoughts. Thoughts then lose their power and are more likely to dissolve both during and beyond meditation.

The busy mind also gives us the opportunity to reconnect with the body; if it makes us feel frustrated we can notice where that feeling of frustration arises in the body and make that a focus of our attention. When we do this we can transform our relationship to thoughts and the feelings that they produce. We teach the mind that actually it is us who is steering the ship. We are also more likely to notice where in the body we carry our tensions; bringing awareness to this can help us improve the way we use our body, potentially overcoming the aches and pains of misuse and heading off injury before it occurs.

To do: notice

Many of us have little obsessions that we may not have noticed before but now suddenly become clear to us. I used to make a constant to-do list in my mind; this same list would go round-and-round making me anxious about all the things which I had to do, making me worry about forgetting something and occupying space in my brain. After meditating for a few months I noticed that this list wasn't there anymore; the information might be in there somewhere but I am not aware of it or the underlying angst it used to create. I do still forget things sometimes but probably less than I used to.

Thinking about stuff doesn't get it done – only getting it done does.

If we teach ourselves not to be subject to the busy mind then we can overcome procrastination, focus more and stop the mind wandering.

Meditation: Bodyscan

Let's try out another meditation.

When you are ready read the below through once and give it a go:

Find your comfortable position, either sitting or lying down. The purpose of this meditation is to connect with your body in the moment, without judging or thinking about it, just feeling it.

Take a few deep breaths and relax into where you are. If any thoughts arise just watch them come and go again.

Start at the very top of your head and scan slowly downwards through your body, feel each area of your body:

The very top of your head on the outside
The top of your head on the inside of your skull
Moving down into your forehead
Your right temple
The back of your head
Your left temple
Your left eye
The bridge of your nose
Your right eye

Continue this taking your time in your own way down through the entire body. Let thoughts come and go, returning your attention all the time to your body in a relaxed awareness. If you forget where you were just return to the last place you can remember. Try not to rush, just be wherever you are in the body.

You can do this with the freedom of taking your own time or if you feel more comfortable using a timer you can do so, but try to give yourself enough time to fit in the whole body thoroughly. The more in-depth you are longer the meditation will be; when you have done the entire body once you can start again at the top of the head sweeping downwards more quickly and repeat for the length of your meditation. Try around 10 minutes for your first go and increase to a time that is suitable for you as you develop your practice.

Beginner's Mind

Each moment is a new beginning, every day a new life.

The principle of beginner's mind reminds us to begin again exactly where we are. We do this in meditation, every time we lose our way or get tangled up in thought – we notice and just begin again. We start over, finding this breath, uncovering the gateway back to right where we are. So much beauty hidden in plain sight; just here, just now where the action always is.

And so we begin to begin again in life. From lost to found as we feel our step like the first we've ever taken.

We get to fall in love with life again by embracing the art of new beginnings. A freshness and vibrancy shines from beyond the familiar.

Learn the language of happiness

You are learning a new language and if you want to become fluent you are going to have to practise a little bit every day. If you do you will soon reach a point where it feels natural; rather than another task to tick off that list, meditation becomes an integral part of our life.

Everyone wants to be happy but you need to be prepared to do something about it. You really can retrain your mind to be tuned into the joy that is all around you. If you wanted a six-pack you'd have to do a lot of sit-ups; this is far less strenuous than that.

Turning inside out

We always look to things outside of ourselves to make us happy. The last thing we want to hear is that happiness is within us, particularly if we don't have a good relationship with ourselves and allow our thoughts to run our lives.

Our thoughts say, 'This is all a load of rubbish, this isn't the answer, you'll never be happy or you'll only be happy when...'

The difference is that now you can see you are separate from those thoughts, somehow you can watch them from a distance. You can choose to go with them and believe them if you want, maybe you are just not done with all of your suffering yet.

At some point when you are ready to give up and say, 'I have been through enough,' that's when you will be ready to embrace what is right here. Some people never get the chance, they die full of rumination and regret – if only someone had told them to watch their breath and to pay attention to their life in the moments that it unfolded.

Life in boxes

We like to stick areas of our lives into boxes…

Bad box
Boring box
Good box

We run away from the bad stuff, ignore the boring stuff and chase the good stuff.

If we lose the labels and just try to experience what is going on in this moment, whatever this may be, we wake up to the fullness of life, find joy in all things and realise that even the bad stuff might not all be as terrible as our minds would convince us.

Find the happiness in each moment

There is beauty in all things if you absorb yourself in the act of whatever it is you are doing. This day-to-day beauty is your life. Happiness will not arrive when some far-off goal is achieved, but will arise when you notice all the joy that surrounds you.

Drinking, eating, brushing your teeth, putting your shoes on, listening to the birds, listening to the clock ticking. The feeling of my fingers on this keypad. Washing up – the bubbles, the temperature of the water. The sound of a boiling kettle. Having a shower and feeling the drops of water hit your body – the smell of the soap, how it feels to have clean hair. Walking in the sunshine, walking in the rain, just walking – the feel of the ground beneath your feet, of grass between your toes or sand or the ocean. The roar of the sea going in and out like the earth breathing, the gentle trickle of a stream, the splash when you walk through a puddle.

We might practise paying attention while we are sitting down in our quiet moments of meditation but it is the mindful bringing of attention to all that we do that this is a rehearsal for.

Mindful Moments

Pick something you will do mindfully today.
Small and simple is usually the best way to start.

Today for instance I will mindfully make a cup of tea. I will really absorb myself in the whole process: the sounds, smells and sensations of the entire act right through to my first sip. I may choose to do this just once or use making tea as my cue to be mindful with each cup I make.

If we start with one little thing to do mindfully then over time add in other small opportunities to be mindful, soon enough we find our day becomes a dot-to-dot of these moments. Then after a while we start joining the dots to create a whole new picture of our lives.

Never wait again, what is it you are waiting for?

Make waiting a time for meditation, the perfect opportunity to 'check in' with yourself, to breathe, to be in your body and find some clarity rather than letting the mind run rings around you.

Stuck in a traffic jam – what are your options? You can either get really stressed out or give in to the moment, choosing not to be stressed; either way you are still not going anywhere fast. If you can train your mind to swap waiting for 'being' and accept the things you cannot change then you transform your experience of everyday annoyances. All of a sudden the world that was turning against you is flowing in the same direction that you are.

Does the world need to be different for you to be happy or do you need to approach it differently? Who are you fighting against? There is no point fighting the tide, it will go in and it will go back out again; once you accept this you can literally live your life in the flow. That doesn't mean a lack of purpose or ambition reigns, just that you pick your battles more wisely; once you have the clarity of mindfulness in your life you can distinguish what is worth striving for.

Letting go of stresses that are not worth your energy leaves far more vigour for those things which really need it. When you don't have the weight of battle armour on every day all sorts of opportunities open up, we stop waiting for something amazing to happen and realise that it is already taking place. People, connections and ideas that may have been sitting just under our nose for years we suddenly become 'aware' of.

Being mindful is easy, it's just remembering to be mindful that's the tricky part but we can do this through practice; that starts now.

Building up your practice

We are where we are; meditation is not another stick to beat yourself with, life can be busy and lead us in all sorts of different directions, that's kind of the point.

Along my own journey I have been intimidated and a bit put off by teachers who insisted you sit and meditate for long stretches every day without fail. Be kind to yourself and work something realistic into your life that is going to work for you. It is far better to do a little bit every day than heaps once every now and again. Make meditation your new habit – start small and build upwards, I started on just 10 minutes a day and definitely felt a real difference from doing this consistently; some is definitely better than none. Once you get into the habit you will notice how horrible you are if there is a day you miss; know yourself and this should be all the motivation you need. The ideal practice is the one that you actually do but certainly if you can fit in 20–30 minutes of practice a day you will quickly see huge changes in the way you feel; the more you manage to fit in the better. If you have the time set a timer for 45 minutes and enjoy the transformative impact this can have!

Meditation: Counting the Out-breath

Many people find the act of counting the breath really helpful to stay focused particularly when they are new to meditation. Once you have improved your ability to focus in this way you may want to try to see if you can stretch yourself to remain focused without such a strict anchor. Once you are managing to count each breath from 1–10 without getting distracted about 80–90% of the time, try counting the out-breaths only, this gives you some extra space to enjoy, which when you are ready for it can feel really blissful.

Same as before just focus on the breaths and watch any thoughts come and then go without having to engage with them.

If you do find yourself really distracted then go back to counting both the in- and the out-breath until that settles down and then move back to just the out-breaths again if and when you are ready.

It is not a rush or race to be able to do this, please try to not get frustrated; just enjoy being at the stage you are at and the process of training your incredible brain.

Set your intention

Meditation gives us a starting point; you may get a bit mad again during the course of the day but the state of meditation brings you back to the moment.

Meditation is setting aside a bit of time to be exactly where you are.

We don't meditate to get good at meditation, we meditate to be awake to life.

Meditation: Following the Breath

The next step once you have spent some time retraining your mind to stay focused with just counting the out-breath is to lose the counting altogether and just follow the breath.

When you are ready read the below through once and give it a go:

Feel your breath.

It is the force that is always there, wherever we go, whatever we do, whoever we 'think' we are.

Just feel it, going in and out of the body.

Give it your full attention, feel its quality; the connection between the internal and the external world.

The breath is the life-giving force that is no different in us than in any other human or mammal. In breathing we are all the same.

Feel the point the breath enters and where it reaches in the body. What is its texture? Its temperature? Does it have a smell? How does it feel? How does it make your nostrils feel? And the rest of your nose? How does it feel going into your chest, and as the lungs expand what happens to the rest of your body?

Focus on this for a few minutes and in the moment that you realise your mind may have wandered just gently bring it back to the simple task of watching the breath.

To have the mind full of the breath is the key to meditation, the key to mindfulness and ultimately the key to happiness.

There are lots of other techniques and layers which can be added but the simple act of following the breath is your essential and effective way to connect with the present; it is your anchor to 'now'.

Meditation is really easy; it is something you automatically know how to do, it is something you have actually used hundreds of times before and not necessarily been aware of it. It is those moments when your mind is full of what you are doing, where you are yourself.

Make time for happiness

A big obstacle your thoughts will throw at you is, 'I don't have time to meditate.'

If you genuinely don't have time for happiness in your life maybe you need to change your life.

If most of us think of all the hours we have wasted on worry or regret then this puts time spent meditating into context. That was the past, we can do nothing about it but we can change now to make all worry a thing of the past and meditation is one of the ways we can do this.

Transform your view of others

Recognise that people are carrying around the weight of the world on their shoulders, that they are lost in their thoughts, their fears, their anger, their projections of who they are and who you are in relation to them – this is not truly them, it's just their egos so don't get drawn in. This can be so hard, especially when it is people we know and love, but your consciousness can bring about a change in them. Your awareness will cause a change in your responses and in turn their reactions will shift in time.

We see people walking down the street, clearly lost in their own inner world, full of anger and not noticing anything that's going on around them. You never need be that person again; you have been liberated from all that madness.

Everything Changes

Life will happen, time will pass and each moment is unique.

Make a habit of watching the changing mind. You may tell yourself or others, 'I am always miserable/angry/sad/lonely etc...' however, if you watch the mind you can train yourself to notice when the emotion arises and when it falls away again. This can be really liberating, for when we see that how we feel is fluid and ever changing we are less hard on ourselves and less frightened of our emotions.

When we feel an emotion rising in ourselves rather than fuel it with the usual thoughts that surround it – 'Oh no, here I go again feeling lonely, I'm never going to meet anyone, I'm going to grow old and no one will ever love me, I'll be eaten by my own cats etc.' – we can instead watch it, note it and choose not to fuel it. We do this not by running away from the feeling but by feeling it physically.

Read the example below and then try it out for yourself the next time you feel an emotion rising in you:

I have had some thoughts around loneliness and can feel this has caused an emotion to arise in the body.

My chest feels tight and there is an ache across the back of my shoulders and around my heart.

I concentrate on the feeling rather than the thoughts surrounding them. When I notice the urge to engage in thinking I bring myself back to the feeling and my breath.

I experience the fullness of the feeling and thoughts just come and go.

I don't run away from the feeling, I stick with it.

Then the feeling starts to change, it begins to move away from my chest and starts to dissolve.

Underneath this is calm and relief.

Suspending the story of 'me'

We build up a picture of ourselves based on all that has gone before in our lives and define ourselves by this.

Everything we are taught from an early age points to us forming a sense of identity and an importance on knowing who we are; this is something we often buy into and get ourselves tangled up in.

When we become mindful of our thoughts we reveal to ourselves that our history is a story that we tell ourselves and anyone who'll listen, and that this story changes depending on who we are telling and how we feel. Once we learn to separate ourselves from the story we can also separate ourselves from the roles we have created within it be they baddie, hero, victim, slave or whatever. Once we no longer embody these roles a world of possibilities opens itself up to us because suddenly it dawns on us that we don't know how the story ends after all.

Accept that you have no idea who you are and open yourself up to some happily ever after…

All we can know is now.

Be true to yourself

That sounds really corny but many of us don't know who our true self is because we have built up so many layers of bullshit and backstory over the years. We get so consumed with the versions of ourselves which we present to people and what in turn they think about us that we no longer know what the authentic version of ourselves is. This is all ego. Being in-the-moment is losing your ego. Losing your ego doesn't make you less funny or brilliant, it just makes you more you. Most people are scared that they are not as good as the version of themselves they work so hard to maintain but once we lose the ego and all its analysis, criticism and time wasting, we have the capacity to be infinitely better and more brilliant than we could have imagined.

Don't believe your hype

Uncover your patterns of self-sabotage by watching your mind.

Oh how the mind loves to create drama, something juicy to chew on and distract us from the life that is happening right in front of our eyes. When we are unconscious of this our gaze projects outwards so it is often easy to see these patterns in others rather than ourselves. If we instead turn that focus inwards we start to pick up on those patterns and reveal how we have developed behaviours which make us our own worst enemy.

Many of these patterns are based on underlying beliefs that we have picked up on our journey through life and take as truisms when in reality they are nonsense.

Whenever things were going well in my life I used to suddenly get this overwhelming feeling of dread because I knew something really awful was just about to happen, a belief that with every good thing you must pay for with a bad one. When you break this down that is the belief of a child, probably something I had picked up at 4 or 5, but unless we stand back and create enough distance between our thoughts and beliefs and the reality of what is really happening in our lives how can we ever work out what is the truth for ourselves.

Take some quiet time and you can quite literally strip layers off of yourself, baggage you have been lugging around for a lifetime without even realising.

... I'm never happy... I'll never be happy... relationships never work out... everyone in our family gets depression so it's just my destiny... etc, etc, etc.

Lose it, take it off, you don't need it, it is just thought and it is not helpful.

Change your world

When we change ourselves the reflection of the world we are projecting changes; transforming hell into heaven, not in some projected future but now.
This is the key to liberation, freedom, happiness.

Make an intention to smile more today and watch that ripple back to you in the faces of those you encounter. Let's mindfully begin a reflective revolution.

It's OK

We spend much of our lives running from strong emotion, hiding locked up in our heads, battling within ourselves so that we don't have to face how we feel, numbing this with alcohol and drugs, distracting ourselves with television, but actually when we face and accept the energy of feelings they can be transformed.

If you are in pain go within – focus on the feeling of pain, not the thoughts of pain.

Give it your full attention, find out where it is in the body and really feel it, sit with it, face it, don't turn away but truly let the force of the emotion come to you. Through this you are able to transform pain; it is not something which can be described, only felt.

Allow yourself to meditate on your pain and transform your life.

Life is beautiful,
Miraculous,
Incredible.
Don't fight it or resist it,
Let it be.

Meditation: The Power of Attention

Where we place our attention becomes biggest and brightest to us. This is no secret, just listen and hear the truth of all things for yourself.

You may find it helpful to read a line, place your attention on that one area and then close your eyes to really draw in all of your focus.

Placing as much attention as you can on...

The sounds inside the room you are sitting in; what can you hear? Does the sound have a quality, pitch or tone. Listen into it, feel into it.

The ticking of a clock, creaks of pipes or furniture, the movement of a fan. Notice what you are noticing and really give the sound you are noticing the fullness of your attention.
Breathe.

Is there an underlying buzz or hum in the room itself?

Can you hear the sound of your own breathing?

Can you hear the beating of your heart?

Rest your attention on what you are noticing for a few moments and really dive into the sensations of this.

Notice if your attention moves elsewhere.
Notice how it is possible to observe the attention drifting and how it is possible to move your awareness into something else.

Your attention is yours to give, be aware of where you choose to place it.

Feel into the tips of your toes, now the soles of your feet – is there any tingling, fizzing or sensation here? Rest your awareness here. Unconscious flitting of attention robs us of one of our greatest assets; bring your attention into the light of awareness and see how it is possible to illuminate your experience of life in a new way.

Now, gently move your attention to the sounds outside the room. What can you hear? What are you drawn to? Focus on a single sound and witness how this makes it appear louder.

Can you feel the aliveness of your body? The breeze on your skin? Layers of taste and touch and sensation? As you focus on this, observe how the intensity of taste increases, how sensation is heightened.

Rest in this awareness, observing the power of your attention for as long as you would like; come back to me when you are ready. I'll meet you on the next page.

Your life is the creation of your focus

As you will have seen from the meditation on the previous page, focusing on something turns up its impact and volume. That which we focus on we get more of.

This is what we do in every area of our lives. It is easy to get tangled up in rotations of repetitive thought; the more attention we give these the stronger the pull of those well-trodden pathways of the mind. Retraining attention to the present is the secret to breaking these cycles. In the instant we return to ourselves, we make the now come to life: suddenly the simplest of things is filled with a vibrancy, the smallest interaction resonates in a more meaningful way. Like tuning the radio to a different frequency, we can stand in the same room but hear a new song by harnessing the power of our attention.

Who are you?

You are not a CV, you are not a history of things that might have happened to you or a list of things you hope or fear will.

Does who you think you are get in the way of who you really are?

Once you accept the moment and become conscious of who you are rather than who you 'thought' you were everything changes.

When you move into this 'consciousness' the walls of the prison of your mind dissolve, boundaries and barriers that your mind created are no longer there, it is like you are seeing for the first time and possibilities are infinite.

Time no longer exists and energy and space take on new meaning, you are high on life.

Once you have seen this and are aware, there is no going back; you may forget for a bit and let your thoughts slip back in, but underneath you will know who you are and how it is. You choose how to use this knowledge, whether to develop it or try to ignore it and stick with the status quo, but you will know and you will be drawn to return to 'consciousness'.

Carry awareness into your everyday life; make it your everyday life.

Meditation: Who am I?

When you are ready read this through and have a go:

Slowly... step by step...

Go through a bodyscan

Take some time counting the breath

When you are ready switch to just counting the out-breaths

When this feels comfortable just let the counting fall away and follow the breath

When you feel ready let the concentrated focus on breath fall away and just be present in the space where you are

Ask 'Who am I?'

At first it is likely that many ripples of thought occur – just watch them and allow them to come and go, then after a while things may start bubbling up to the surface from deep down below. Just be there and experience what happens.

Give it a go.

Serendipity

Through paying attention to what is going on both in us and around us we are far more ready to stumble upon things which can improve our lives; big or little things, these accidental discoveries can bring great joy and pleasure.

Happiness is just a moment away (it's in this moment too). Do you believe that some people just get their 'lucky break' in life or is it that they are aware of opportunities that arise, that they are open to people and experiences rather than lost in thought?

Your Universal Nature

There are more brain cells in your head than there are stars in our galaxy.

If we close our eyes with the same wonder as looking up at the night sky we might glimpse the universe that exists inside of us.

Universe (uni-verse: one-song); a single everchanging symphony in which we are both the dancer and the dance. Like lovers entwined we get so close we disappear.

The Secret Magic of Mindfulness: Now Is The Time For Happiness

With words we are always casting a spell (that's why it's called spelling).

Be mindful of what you are 'spelling' both outwardly and in. Words may be just labels but they point towards feeling, acting as signposts on the map of our lives. They can lead us downward along narrow pathways or lift us up into the light. Awareness is the key to unlocking the power of words, once we begin really listening we hear in a new way.

Shine brightly in your knowing

If all you do is read this book or all I do is write it, the words spelt out are simply thoughts.

Magic happens in the moment something truly resonates with us, we feel it in our being, we know our truth. We remember who we really are.

You have arrived at your destination; you know the secret magic of mindfulness.

Now is the time for happiness.

A Final Note from Frances

If you are reading this then we are connected and I feel so grateful to be sharing these moments with you. Thank you. Wherever you are on your own path, to look beyond the norm and within ourselves is one of the most challenging, and yet, important steps we can choose to take. This is the hero's Journey.

Here we have an opportunity to spread something quite incredible. What would the world look like if everyone realised they are not their thoughts? If people were not so lost in their own stories but were living a mindfully aware life. How could the ripples of that knowing change the shape of human history and our beautiful planet?

When we live in thought we act from fear, when we know who we truly are we act from love.

Please help me spread the love however you can,

Much love, Frances x

How to Access Guided Meditation Recordings

Free Stuff! Mindfulness for everyone, everywhere… my team and I have dedicated many hours to recording and editing meditations and teachings for you to enjoy and share.

To access our guided meditations please subscribe to the Mindfully Happy Podcast. Once you 'subscribe' to this free resource you'll have access to a whole range of meditation recordings including varying lengths of the meditations found within this book, plus many more.

You can access this via the link:
http://mindfully.libsyn.com/podcast

You can also do so via any smartphone or tablet, just search for 'Podcasts', then within this search 'Mindfully Happy Meditations with Frances Trussell'.

How to Connect with Frances

Please do connect with me on Social Media. I really look forward to you joining our community.

Instagram:
https://www.instagram.com/francestrussellmindfullyhappy/

Facebook:
https://www.facebook.com/mindfullyhappywithfrancestrussell/

Twitter:
https://twitter.com/FrancesTrussell

YouTube: search 'Mindfully Happy' for our YouTube Channel

You can also link to these via: www.francestrussell.com and www.mindfullyhappy.com

Acknowledgements

A massive thank you…

To all of my students – you have been the most incredible teachers and I feel so grateful to have met you all, a thousand beautiful faces flash through my mind. Thank you for helping me refine my material and know beyond doubt that this works; do the practice and life transforms.

To all those that have taught and inspired me, there have been many of you. In particular Daizan Roshi, your time, patience and 'pointing' skills have been invaluable, thank you so much for all that you have dedicated your life to doing. The team at Zenways and their incredible enlightenment intensives. Thank you to Gaunts House for providing such a special space. Paul Vallins for teaching me through laughter, Adrian Rides and the Now team. To Marisa Peer for giving me such confidence and helping me let go of limitations. To Dan Turner for creating the Mindfully Happy Podcast. To Joe Pasquale for 'everything', those serendipities let us know we are on the right path.

To all of my family for being wonderful. The amazing Grace and Harrison for being natural zen masters (you can't really teach kids mindfulness, but you can learn from them). To Kevin for all of your love and support, this book would not have been possible without it. To everyone whose help has enabled me to write and retreat particularly Mum and Alan, Elizabeth and Tom, Dad and Leigh and the very special Helen Crowe.

To Kate Rowlandson for believing in my writing and for introducing me to John Hunt and Team who I thank for getting this published. To Olivia Buxton for helping me reach people.

To Alex Joicey and Carlise Jones, along with Adele and all at the Mindful Living Show. To my remarkable bunch of friends who support me and sing my praises even when my own inner critic runs wild – too many of you to mention but you know who you are and I love you all very much.

Train with Frances Trussell

www.francestrussell.com

frances@mindfullyhappy.com

Your Space

Notes, Meditation Insights and Mindful Musings...

About the Author

Frances Trussell MA, PGDIP, BA, C.HYP, MPMH

Frances Trussell lives in lovely Hampton Court, just outside London, with her husband and two very mindful little people, her children: Grace and Harrison. She is passionate about making mindfulness accessible to all and has taught mindfulness meditation to many hundreds of people in a range of settings.

Her client base delights in diversity including high profile stars and CEO's, builders and stay-at-home parents, school children to mature clients in their 90's and a vibrant mixture of everyone in-between. Her experience has taught her that whatever stage we are in life, or however we define ourselves, we all face the same human challenges and can help ourselves to have a richer experience through mindfulness.

Frances is a mindfulness advisor on TV, in schools, to charities and across the corporate world. A pioneer of Mindfulness-based Rapid Transformational Therapy in her 1-1 work, she helps clients to quickly overcome anxiety and depression so that they can be more present in their lives.

Writing, mindfulness and dancing are what makes Frances 'come alive'.

She is founder of Mindfully Happy www.mindfullyhappy.com which provides mindfulness training to groups and individuals. You can find out more about Frances at www.francestrussell.com.

BOOKS

O-BOOKS

SPIRITUALITY

O is a symbol of the world, of oneness and unity; this eye represents knowledge and insight. We publish titles on general spirituality and living a spiritual life. We aim to inform and help you on your own journey in this life.

If you have enjoyed this book, why not tell other readers by posting a review on your preferred book site? Recent bestsellers from O-Books are:

Heart of Tantric Sex
Diana Richardson
Revealing Eastern secrets of deep love and intimacy to Western couples.
Paperback: 978-1-90381-637-0 ebook: 978-1-84694-637-0

Crystal Prescriptions
The A-Z guide to over 1,200 symptoms and their healing crystals
Judy Hall
The first in the popular series of six books, this handy little guide is packed as tight as a pill-bottle with crystal remedies for ailments.
Paperback: 978-1-90504-740-6 ebook: 978-1-84694-629-5

Take Me To Truth
Undoing the Ego
Nouk Sanchez, Tomas Vieira
The best-selling step-by-step book on shedding the Ego, using the teachings of *A Course In Miracles*.
Paperback: 978-1-84694-050-7 ebook: 978-1-84694-654-7

The 7 Myths about Love...Actually!
The journey from your HEAD to the HEART of your SOUL
Mike George
Smashes all the myths about LOVE.
Paperback: 978-1-84694-288-4 ebook: 978-1-84694-682-0

The Holy Spirit's Interpretation of the New Testament
A course in Understanding and Acceptance
Regina Dawn Akers
Following on from the strength of *A Course In Miracles*, NTI teaches us how to experience the love and oneness of God.
Paperback: 978-1-84694-085-9 ebook: 978-1-78099-083-5

The Message of A Course In Miracles
A translation of the text in plain language
Elizabeth A. Cronkhite
A translation of *A Course in Miracles* into plain, everyday language for anyone seeking inner peace. The companion volume, *Practicing A Course In Miracles*, offers practical lessons and mentoring.
Paperback: 978-1-84694-319-5 ebook: 978-1-84694-642-4

Thinker's Guide to God
Peter Vardy
An introduction to key issues in the philosophy of religion.
Paperback: 978-1-90381-622-6

Your Simple Path
Find happiness in every step
Ian Tucker
A guide to helping us reconnect with what is really important in
our lives.
Paperback: 978-1-78279-349-6 ebook: 978-1-78279-348-9

365 Days of Wisdom
Daily Messages To Inspire You Through The Year
Dadi Janki
Daily messages which cool the mind, warm the heart and guide
you along your journey.
Paperback: 978-1-84694-863-3 ebook: 978-1-84694-864-0

Readers of ebooks can buy or view any of these bestsellers by
clicking on the live link in the title. Most titles are published
in paperback and as an ebook. Paperbacks are available in
traditional bookshops. Both print and ebook formats are
available online.

Find more titles and sign up to our readers' newsletter at
http://www.johnhuntpublishing.com/mind-body-spirit

Follow us on Facebook at https://www.facebook.com/OBooks/
and Twitter at https://twitter.com/obooks

albums often finish up in a box in the loft, taking up valuable space and scarcely looked at. You have your memories in your mind and in your heart. Holding on to the physical reminders can often keep us from moving on and living in the present.

- Sell unwanted items on online sites. (Please refer to the Further Reading and Multimedia List for more information.)

Upcycling

There is no denying that we live in a throwaway culture. Where once goods were made to last, corporations soon caught on to the idea of *planned obsolescence,* that of giving a product an artificially limited useful life, using cheaper component parts which were planned to deteriorate more quickly. This generates greater sales in the long run, as the time between repeat purchases is reduced. Fashion trends in media outlets (television, magazines, advertising etc.) perpetuate this idea of continually buying newer (better?) products, as does the search for happiness, which many of us undertake, in the accumulation of possessions. However, an item soon loses its shine, its charm or its use and we seek to replace it with a newer, glossier version.

I have recently started to pay attention to the 'absolute poverty' in some developing countries as compared to our 'relative poverty' in the richer countries of the Western world. Absolute poverty is the level below which no-one in the world should live—not having the most basic amounts of what are the essentials in life, such as water, food, shelter, and having to survive on a paltry amount of money (in some cases $1) per day. Relative poverty refers to those who fall below the higher minimum income standards of that country in relation to the average. When faced with the inequalities of resources in the world (money, food, water, land and so on) our consumerism in the West seems pointless. We have everything we need. We don't need any more. So what can we do from home to upcycle in order to disembark from the consumerist train? Here are some ideas:

Repaint items. Old metal-framed mirror wardrobe doors are rejuvenated when painted white to match woodwork, then using glass frosting spray to frost all or parts of the glass. Wooden picture frames can be repainted to match the color of a feature wall in any room. Look at an object in your home which has lost its shine. Now, use your imagination and think: Instead of replacing it with new, could it be repainted or embellished?

Modify items. Give them new purpose. There are many websites and books which outline upcycling and crafting ideas. Please see the Further Reading and Multimedia List at the back for my recommendations. Crafts are seeing a resurgence in popularity in the UK, from knitting to dressmaking, jewelry-making to decoupage and so on.

My niece made a Christmas snow globe from an old glass jar, something she had learned at a crafting class. You can find instructions for how to do this on online sites.

Use old fruit crates or wooden boxes to make a horizontal garden outside your window. I have seen expensive versions of these in DIY stores but why not make your own?

Buy upcycled goods made from coffee sacks or paper, for example. This year, I was sent a Christmas tree decoration of a robin. It was made from recycled paper by a women's fair-trade company in the Philippines. By buying recycled or upcycled goods we may also be helping to sustain smaller, local enterprises, mostly not-for-profit, in countries around the world. In this way you are effecting change by spreading kindness on a global scale.

Re-gift unwanted gifts. If you feel uneasy about doing this, then donate them to local charity shops or give them to loved ones at any time of year, and not for their birthday or at Christmas time.

Buy fabric dyes to revamp clothes. Use a large spare plastic container to dye clothes or store other items.

Don't buy new. What if we set ourselves the challenge of not buying anything new for our homes for a month! Could we manage it? Would we be prepared to take on this challenge? A first step is being more innovative in our thinking. What is it that is really essential for our daily lives? Stop and pause before you buy. Leave it for a day. Perhaps tomorrow you won't see the need for it after all.

My friend and I decided not to spend money on clothes for a year unless it was essential. We found it gratifying to only buy three new items that year. This theme could be further developed by reshaping our shopping habits to buy pre-loved clothes (i.e. second-hand) from charity shops and pre-loved clothes boutiques. Hosting a 'swap shop' evening with friends is another fun way to change your look for free.

Conclusion

I said in the Preface to *Acts of Kindness from Your Armchair* that its aim was to explore how the housebound among us may live a spiritual life and make a positive, meaningful contribution to the world through acts of kindness. Kindness, remember, is about allowing love into our hearts so that we may share it with others. The more we practice being and acting kind—to ourselves, to others, to the animal kingdom and to the environment—the more these attributes of kindness will become inherent in our daily lives.

This book teaches that acts of kindness can be big or small but always of equal importance. It has shown how vital it is to work on ourselves first in order to remove any blocks, any unhelpful inner motivations or prejudices. By embarking on our own spiritual development in the first instance, by thinking of and putting others first above ourselves with no thought of reward, it is at this point that we discover a limitless number of acts of kindness within ourselves which we already—and can—do now.

I have sought to share the spiritual knowledge and practical skills gained in recent years and which have been, and continue to be, of great benefit to me. Reading the book is the starting point regardless of where you are on your spiritual journey. It takes daily practice to retrain our minds with new, positive habits of behavior and thinking.

Acts of Kindness from Your Armchair has presented you with many opportunities and ideas to enable a shift in focus from 'inward-looking' to 'outward-acting,' to see that acts of kindness are not only big, visible acts but the simple, innate thoughts, words and acts of kindness within us all. I hope you will see that your love and kindness are the threads which bind the tapestry of the planet together. All different, each one separate, and yet all connected one to the other, all part of the Whole.

Allowing love and kindness to come to the forefront of our lives reconnects us to the world, dissipating any feelings of isolation or separateness. An awareness that we all have our challenges to face on Earth; that all life on the planet is interconnected; that our ego is the source of most of our unhappiness; all of these things make for a deep spiritual shift from selfishness to selflessness. We will be known for our goodwill, our benevolence and understanding of others. We will be known as charitable, compassionate and non-judgmental. We will feel the generosity and humanity in our hearts. We will see reflected in the eyes of others our kindliness and our compassion.

Through reading *Acts of Kindness from Your Armchair* you may have found a greater degree of peace and purpose in your heart. By carrying out selfless acts of kindness to others, to animals and to the environment, you learn to truly love yourself in the process. Bless you. I wish you joy.

I leave you with a poem from me to remind you of the journey you have undertaken.

Kindness
When you love without, you thrive within
When you care for others
Your Soul is swaddled
In the arms of the Creator.
Each ripple of your compassion
Fills the Infinite Ocean.
Each step you take
To connect with your neighbor
Lightens and brightens your inner demeanor.

No longer will you walk on by, but notice and act.
No longer will you make others cry,
But embrace them instead with the
Endless reach of your love.
At each moment,
Recall our Interconnectedness
Remember that We are One.
In this moment,
Know that you are amazing
A blessing from above.
In every moment,
May you choose kindness and love.

Further Reading and Multimedia List

Here are some of my recommendations for further reading:

Books

Byrne, Rhonda. *The Magic.* Simon & Schuster: UK, 2012.

Ehrmann, Max. *Desiderata.* 1926.

Kindred Spirit Magazine, Watkins Publishing: UK.

Lake, Gina. *Radiance: Experiencing Divine Presence.* Amazon Publishing: UK, 2006.

Morrison, Deborah and Arvind Singh. *Nexus.* Manor House Publishing Inc.: Canada, 2006.

Permutt, Philip. *The Complete Guide to Crystal Chakra Healing.* Cico Books. UK, 2009.

Virtue, Doreen. *How to Hear Your Angels.* Hay House Publishing: UK, 2007.

MacCuish, Savitri, Dr Mansukh Patel and John Jones. *Walking with the Bhagavad Gita.* Life Foundation Publications: UK, 1998.

Apps

Cali, John. *Spirit Oracle Cards.* IndieGoes Software.

Harrold, Glenn. *Solfeggio Meditation Apps.* Diviniti Publishing: www.hypnosisaudio.com

Relax and Rest; Simply Be. www.meditationoasis.com

Insight timer meditation app. Spotlight Six Software LLC (from Play Store)

Websites

http://anitaneilson.com (my blog Healing Word
www.facebook.com/anitaneilson61 (my Facebook site)
www.bbc.co.uk (for *Springwatch* and *Autumnwatch*)
www.beatthemicrobead.org (re. use of microbeads in

cosmetic products)

http://beautynaturals.com (for natural cosmetic and cleaning products)

www.crowdfunder.co.uk/arbolivia (for sustainable forestry project)

https://www.dogstrust.org.uk

www.ebay.co.uk (online selling site; there are many others to choose from)

www.etsy.com/uk (for recycled paper products from producers around the world)

www.foodawarecic.org.uk

www.greenbrands.co.uk (for natural cleaning products)

www.gumtree.com (local online selling site; there are many others to choose from)

www.hollandandbarrett.com (for cruelty-free products)

www.independent.co.uk (*i* newspaper online)

www.livestrong.com (re. effects of sodium lauryl sulfate etc.)

www.living-lightly.co.uk (re. Spiritual Response Therapy)

www.kindnessblog.com

http://positivenews.org.uk

www.randomactsofkindness.org

www.reiki.org

www.royalmail.com (for online postage)

www.scienceclarified.com

www.spiritualresponse.com

www.upcyclethat.com

https://walkinhershoes.careinternational.org.uk

www.waterwise.org.uk

www.youtube.com (search for: 40 acts of compassion)

AYNI
BOOKS

AYNI BOOKS
ALTERNATIVE HEALTH & HEALING

"Ayni" is a Quechua word meaning "reciprocity" – sharing, giving and receiving – whatever you give out comes back to you. To be in Ayni is to be in balance, harmony and right relationship with oneself and nature, of which we are all an intrinsic part. Complementary and Alternative approaches to health and well-being essentially follow a holistic model, within which one is given support and encouragement to move towards a state of balance, true health and wholeness, ultimately leading to the awareness of one's unique place in the Universal jigsaw of life – Ayni, in fact.

If you have enjoyed this book, why not tell other readers by posting a review on your preferred book site. Recent bestsellers from AYNI Books are:

Reclaiming Yourself from Binge Eating
A Step-By-Step Guide to Healing
Leora Fulvio, MFT
Win the war against binge eating, wake up each morning at peace with your body, unafraid of food and overeating.
Paperback: 978-1-78099-680-6 ebook: 978-1-78099-681-3

The Reiki Sourcebook (revised ed.)
Frans Stiene, Bronwen Stiene
A popular, comprehensive and updated manual for the Reiki novice, teacher and general reader.
Paperback: 978-1-84694-181-8 ebook: 978-1-84694-648-6

The Chakras Made Easy
Hilary H. Carter
From the successful Made Easy series, *Chakras Made Easy* is a practical guide to healing the seven chakras.
Paperback: 978-1-78099-515-1 ebook: 978-1-78099-516-8

The Inner Heart of Reiki
Rediscovering Your True Self
Frans Stiene
A unique journey into the inner heart of the system of Reiki, to help practitioners and teachers rediscover their True Selves.
Paperback: 978-1-78535-055-9 ebook: 978-1-78535-056-6

Middle Age Beauty
Soulful Secrets from a Former Face Model Living Botox Free in Her Forties
Machel Shull
Find out how to look fabulous during middle age without plastic surgery by learning inside secrets from a former model.
Paperback: 978-1-78099-574-8 ebook: 978-1-78099-575-5

Readers of ebooks can buy or view any of these bestsellers by clicking on the live link in the title. Most titles are published in paperback and as an ebook. Paperbacks are available in traditional bookshops. Both print and ebook formats are available online.

Find more titles and sign up to our readers' newsletter at
http://www.johnhuntpublishing.com/mind-body-spirit
Follow us on Facebook at https://www.facebook.com/OBooks
and Twitter at https://twitter.com/obooks

You're thinking my star's too cold to seed,
   a black berg of self. Don't press
me on this, I've hours of work before I even start,
   alone with all the crap
I have to sort, the tricks I've played upon
   myself and you – like any son.

and fringes mine, the unillumined space
　　beyond the book of hours'
margins where love without gravity or air
　　fights to pull off its tricks.
Withdrawing to the front lounge during
　　one such interlude, I press
the TV channel changer's power button,
　　browsing toxic Christmas crap
until I hit the news, all contact lost
　　with elderly space-crock Mir, star-
station Lada, emptily afloat,
　　its solar panels turning from the Sun

in a festive sulk, rehearsing with its
　　one last throb of power a reason
to spiral madly to Earth. Disaster movies,
　　billed for primetime hours,
trail from within themselves a pendant
　　gem of romance, like a star
furiously beautiful. Later I relish
　　Kate Winslet's borrowed tart's tricks,
nude on a couch with the *Cœur de la mer*
　　round her neck, posing for a crap
sketch in charcoals by Leonardo DiCaprio.
　　I don't remember press

on board, only the string quartet fiddling
　　to catastrophe, but any press-
man would have had his reflex purged of
　　meaning like an egotistical sun
without planets or my mother memorising
　　her purpose from a scrap
of paper, over and over. Fallen from time,
　　she fights the solid hours.
Downstairs we watch *Titanic*, feel the darkness
　　swamp us when our tricks
of shelter fail and all our spry dependencies
　　shrink back into their star.